Taming The Chaos: Business Owner's Journey to Clarity

Clifford Woods

Published by Clifford Woods, 2024.

While every precaution has been taken in the preparation of this book, the publisher assumes no responsibility for errors or omissions, or for damages resulting from the use of the information contained herein.

TAMING THE CHAOS: BUSINESS OWNER'S JOURNEY TO CLARITY

First edition. September 20, 2024.

Copyright © 2024 Clifford Woods.

ISBN: 979-8227807823

Written by Clifford Woods.

Taming the Chaos:

Business Owner's Journey to Clarity

Table of Contents

Chapter 1: The Descent into Chaos

Michael Davis, once the ambitious and sharp founder of NextGen Strategies, sat in his office, now barely recognizable from the pristine and organized space it once was. The walls, once adorned with awards and certificates, now felt like they were closing in on him. Stacks of unopened mail littered the floor, invoices long forgotten mingled with urgent project documents, and coffee-stained reports cluttered his desk. The monitor flickered, reminding him of countless unread emails and missed deadlines. The digital hum of notifications had become nothing more than white noise in the background of his collapsing empire.

His eyes, bloodshot from lack of sleep, scanned the chaos. There was a time when his agency was unstoppable. NextGen Strategies had been a powerhouse—a fast-growing, high-demand digital marketing firm that clients begged to work with. They were innovators, pushing boundaries in creative strategy, data-driven marketing, and sleek campaigns. The buzz of success had been intoxicating.

But now, the empire he'd built from the ground up was crumbling before his eyes. Clients that had once raved about his visionary approach were now sending curt emails filled with demands and ultimatums. Michael's phone used to light up with friendly calls—now, every call made his heart pound, each conversation another reminder of how much he'd failed to deliver. His once-bold decisions had been reduced to frantic, last-minute firefighting, each new problem piling on top of the last.

The disorganization wasn't contained to the office. His personal life was unraveling, too. Jenny, his wife of twelve years, had become a stranger to him. Once they'd stayed up late talking about their dreams—about travel, the kids, the future. Now, their conversations were reduced to passive-aggressive exchanges about unpaid bills or missed school events. Michael could feel her pulling away, the space between them growing like a chasm. He couldn't remember the last time they shared a real conversation that wasn't colored by frustration or exhaustion.

"Dinner's in the fridge," was her only message that evening, left on a sticky note by the kitchen counter, as he had rushed out the door for another late-night meeting that didn't go as planned. The house, like his business, was no longer a sanctuary—it was just another place filled with unmet expectations.

Late that night, Michael sat alone at his desk, his head in his hands. The weight of it all—NextGen's collapse, his failing marriage, his sense of self slipping through his fingers—was like a heavy blanket smothering him. Every breath felt labored, every decision impossible. He stared at the screen as a new email notification flashed. Another client, another overdue request, another crisis he couldn't fix. His stomach twisted with familiar anxiety, but he didn't even have the energy to open it.

"How did it get like this?" Michael muttered to the empty room. His voice was hoarse, barely a whisper. Leaning back in his chair, he stared up at the ceiling, his mind racing in a thousand directions but making no progress.

The spiral had started slowly, almost imperceptibly. The first few missed emails, the occasional late payment. Then the bigger cracks started to show—missed project milestones, the departure of key employees, his inability to juggle the relentless demands. The worst part was how familiar it felt. He had been here before, at the edge of ruin, during the early startup days. But back then, there was excitement in the chaos. Now, it was just fear.

The door creaked open, and he barely registered the movement. His COO, Alex, stepped inside, the only person still sticking by his side after so many had jumped ship.

"Michael, you need to go home. You've been here for three days straight," Alex's voice was laced with concern, but it carried an undertone of frustration. Even she, his most loyal ally, was nearing her breaking point.

Michael blinked, as if her words were foreign to him. "I can't leave. There's too much—too much to fix. I'm just trying to catch up."

Alex sighed, stepping further into the room, carefully navigating the debris of his broken systems. She placed a hand on his desk, firm yet sympathetic. "We're past catching up, Michael. This... this is survival mode now. If you don't step back and look at the bigger picture, there won't be a business left to save."

Her words struck like a hammer. Survival mode. Michael hated that term, but it was the bitter truth. NextGen wasn't thriving, it wasn't innovating—it was clawing for air in a sea of problems that he had let spiral out of control. He wanted to fight back, to defend himself, but what could he say? It was all too clear.

He ran a hand through his hair, the exhaustion evident in his every movement. "I just don't know where to start. Every time I try to fix one thing, five more fall apart."

Alex leaned in, her tone softening. "Then maybe it's time to admit we need outside help. You've been trying to do everything yourself. We can't keep this up."

The thought made him bristle. Michael Davis, the founder, the leader, asking for help? It went against everything he stood for. He had built NextGen from nothing—there wasn't a single day he didn't put his blood, sweat, and tears into the business. But now, as he looked around the chaos that had consumed him, he realized that stubbornness might have been his greatest downfall.

Before he could respond, his phone buzzed. Jenny's name flashed across the screen. Michael hesitated, staring at the name for a long moment. The last conversation they'd had ended with her walking out of the room, saying she was "done talking." He wasn't sure what would be left to say.

"Take it," Alex urged, her voice gentle but firm. "Go home. Fix what you can there first. The business will still be here tomorrow."

With a heavy sigh, Michael picked up the phone. "Hey," he said, his voice hollow.

Jenny's voice on the other end was flat. "Michael, we need to talk. I can't do this anymore."

There it was. The moment he'd been dreading. As the words hung in the air, Michael felt something inside him shatter. He looked around at the mess he'd made—at work, at home—and realized he was standing on the precipice of losing everything.

But then, a thought surfaced—dark, but undeniable: *Maybe I already have.*

Chapter 2: The Guide Appears

The following day, Michael Davis woke up feeling like he'd been chewed up and spit out by the relentless machine of his own making. The empire he had built from scratch, NextGen Strategies, was beginning to feel more like a prison than a success story. Emails, voicemails, and a stack of urgent tasks sat waiting for him at the office, each one a silent reminder of the chaos that had taken hold. His desk was a battlefield of contracts, sticky notes, and half-baked strategies that no longer seemed to connect.

Today, though, he made a decision: no office. No meetings. Just... a break. He left his phone behind—an unthinkable act for someone so plugged into the corporate world—and headed out, aimlessly walking the streets of the city.

The sharp cold air bit at his cheeks, a welcome shock that helped clear his mind, if only for a brief moment. He had no destination, just a need to escape the endless spiral of crises he couldn't seem to control. His thoughts bounced between frustration, self-doubt, and a gnawing fear that maybe, just maybe, everything was starting to slip beyond his grasp.

Rounding a corner in the old downtown district, a sliver of calm caught his attention. A small, tucked-away bookstore that seemed out of place amid the towering glass buildings and trendy coffee shops. The wooden sign hanging above the door read in carefully painted letters: *The Tidy Mind*. Odd. He was sure he had never seen it before, and he'd walked this route countless times.

The door was propped open slightly, with a welcoming sign: *Free Coffee Inside.*

Normally, he wouldn't have bothered—there was no time for slow moments like bookstores or free coffee in his world—but today was different. Today, he needed something out of the ordinary. Something that didn't remind him of the avalanche waiting for him back at NextGen.

He stepped inside. The faint creak of the door announced his arrival, and immediately, he was enveloped by the scent of old leather, paper, and freshly brewed coffee. The space was cozy, the lighting soft, casting warm shadows across the meticulously organized shelves that lined the walls. Each book looked like it had a purpose, an order—unlike the clutter he had left behind at his office.

He wandered the narrow aisles, his fingers lightly brushing the spines of the books as he breathed in the quiet. There was a calm here, a stillness that seemed miles away from the world outside.

Then, a voice, soft but deliberate, cut through the silence.

"Looking for something?"

Michael turned to find an elderly man seated behind the counter. He was small, with a full head of silver hair that looked as though it had been neatly combed just minutes before. His wire-rimmed glasses perched precariously on the end of his nose as he looked up from a well-worn book. The man's eyes, though, were sharp and piercing, holding a kind of wisdom that Michael found disarming.

Michael hesitated for a moment. "Not really. Just... taking a break from the chaos," he replied, unsure why he felt compelled to share that much.

The old man's face broke into a gentle, knowing smile. "Chaos? Ah, you must be Michael Davis."

Michael's body went rigid. His heartbeat quickened. *How could this man know my name?*

He swallowed hard, forcing a smile. "I'm sorry, do we know each other?"

The old man chuckled, a soft, almost musical sound. "No, not formally," he said, rising slowly from his chair. "But I make it a point to know when someone is as lost as you are."

Michael took an instinctive step back. "What are you talking about?"

"Lost in your own chaos," the man said, gesturing vaguely toward Michael. "I used to be like you once, drowning in the mess I created in my own business. It almost consumed me. But I found a way out. Now, I help people like you—those who need clarity."

Michael couldn't help but scoff, though it came out weaker than he intended. "Clarity? Look, I'm sure you mean well, but you don't know the first thing about what I'm going through."

The old man nodded, unfazed by the brush-off. "You're right. I don't know your story, but I know the storm you're in. You're standing in the middle of it, and all you see is the rain, the destruction. You can't see the patterns yet. The ways the chaos can be turned into something else—into order."

Michael crossed his arms, feeling a strange mix of irritation and curiosity. "And what, you can help me 'see the patterns?"

The man smiled warmly. "I can help you learn to see what's truly broken—and not just the pieces you think are out of place. My name's Oliver Gray, by the way."

Michael stared at him, unsure whether to laugh or walk out, but something about Oliver's demeanor kept him rooted. "What makes you think I'm 'lost'?" Michael asked, still skeptical.

"You wouldn't be here otherwise," Oliver replied simply, turning and pulling a book from the shelf behind him. "And you wouldn't be listening."

A silence settled between them, and for the first time in weeks, Michael found himself at a loss for words.

"You're right about one thing," Michael admitted, dropping his arms to his side. "Everything feels like it's falling apart. It's like I'm trying to hold onto sand. The more I fight it, the more it slips away."

Oliver leaned in, his eyes twinkling with something—was it understanding? "It's because you're trying to fix it all at once. It doesn't work that way. You don't need to repair everything, Michael. You need to know what's really broken."

The words hit Michael like a punch to the gut, and for a moment, the weight of his own denial became too heavy to bear. He exhaled sharply, running a hand through his hair. "And what if I don't know what's broken? What if I don't know where to start?"

Oliver handed him the book—a slim, leather-bound journal, the kind that seemed to have collected years of wisdom in its pages. "Come back tomorrow," Oliver said, placing a hand gently on Michael's shoulder. "I have something for you. But before we start, you need to be ready to face the truth about yourself and your business. And that's not always an easy thing to do."

Michael looked down at the journal, its weight solid in his hands. "You really think you can help me?"

Oliver's smile widened. "I don't think. I know. But whether or not you're ready for that help... that's up to you."

Michael felt a strange mix of trepidation and curiosity. He wasn't entirely sure what Oliver was offering, but something inside told him that it might be exactly what he needed.

As he stepped back into the cold air, the old man's final words echoed in his mind, filling him with both hope and unease: "Tomorrow, Michael. Tomorrow, we begin."

Chapter 3: The First Impossible Situation

―――

The following day, Michael returned to *The Tidy Mind* feeling a strange mixture of anticipation and apprehension. He had barely spoken a word since stepping into Oliver's minimalist office, the quiet hum of a nearby air purifier adding to the surreal calmness of the space. Oliver, seated behind his clutter-free desk, handed Michael a small, leather-bound book titled *Order in Chaos: A Guide for Business Owners*. The title alone felt like it mocked the disarray his life had become.

"Start here," Oliver said, tapping the cover with a thin finger. "Read it tonight. Tomorrow, we take the first step."

Michael nodded, taking the book but not quite registering the magnitude of what lay ahead. Oliver's cryptic demeanor always left him wondering if the man could read his thoughts. Michael tucked the book under his arm and hurried out, his phone buzzing with more urgent emails than he could process.

That evening, at home, Michael sat in his worn leather chair, the city lights casting faint shadows across the room. He cracked open the book, half expecting generic advice he'd seen countless times before—something about discipline, planning, and efficiency. But the first sentence caught him off guard:

Chaos isn't the enemy. It's fear—the fear that you're not enough, that if you don't control everything, you'll lose everything.

He blinked, reading the words again. They hit with a weight he hadn't anticipated. The truth of it was like a sharp sting. His entire approach to running NextGen Strategies had been founded on this fear—working late into the night, believing that only he could hold it all together. The more he tried to manage, the deeper the chaos seemed to consume him.

As the words sunk in, he thought back to the endless nights, the frantic attempts to stay on top of every detail. Instead of gaining control, he had been smothered by the very thing he sought to dominate.

By the time he closed the book, it was well past midnight, and exhaustion settled over him like a heavy blanket. But this time, there was something different—an unsettling awareness that perhaps he had been fighting the wrong battle all along.

The next morning, Michael entered the office with renewed resolve. He could feel the subtle buzz of the team working away, the usual noise of phones ringing and printers whirring filling the air. His mind focused on one task: tackle the Davis & Co. project. It had been sitting on his to-do list far too long, and the client's frustration had reached the tipping point. If he didn't deliver soon, it could cost him not just the project, but a valuable business relationship.

"This is the impossible situation I need to solve," Michael muttered under his breath as he slid into his chair and opened his laptop.

But as the screen blinked to life, his heart stopped cold. The Davis & Co. file—weeks of work—was nowhere to be found. His desktop, usually a mess of icons and forgotten shortcuts, offered no clues. He frantically searched through his folders, scouring every corner of his digital workspace.

Nothing.

His pulse quickened. He flipped to his cloud storage, hoping he might have saved it there as a backup. Still nothing. Panic set in as a cold sweat crept down his back.

This project was massive. Losing it would be a blow his company might not recover from. He felt the weight of it crushing him, the familiar fear he had read about the night before rearing its ugly head.

He grabbed his phone and dialed Sarah, his project manager. The call barely rang before she picked up.

"Have you seen the Davis & Co. file?" he asked, trying to sound calm but failing miserably.

"I thought you had it last," Sarah replied, her voice tight with concern. "Are you sure it's not in your drive?"

"I've checked everywhere!" His frustration boiled over. "It's like it's vanished."

Michael stood up abruptly, his chair slamming against the desk. He tore through the stacks of papers on his desk, scattering them in every direction. The chaos he thought he could control was swallowing him whole.

Just when he was ready to throw his hands up and admit defeat, Oliver's voice echoed in his mind: *You don't need to fix it all at once. You need to start by seeing what's really broken.*

He paused, taking in the wreckage of his office—the disheveled papers, the blinking lights of unfinished tasks on his screen, the ringing phone he hadn't answered in over an hour. He could feel the same chaos swirling inside him, but this time, he wasn't going to let it control him.

Michael closed his eyes, forcing himself to breathe deeply, to stop the madness for just a moment. As he replayed the events of the last few days, a detail surfaced—he had moved the Davis & Co. file to an external drive for safekeeping, telling himself he'd come back to it later.

His eyes flew open. He dropped to his knees and began rifling through the drawer under his desk, where he dumped old cables, forgotten gadgets, and obsolete documents. The tangle of wires scratched at his skin as he dug through, but after what felt like an eternity, his hand landed on something solid. He pulled out a small, battered external hard drive.

With trembling fingers, Michael plugged it into his laptop. His heart raced as the drive whirred to life, and he held his breath until, at last, the Davis & Co. file appeared on the screen.

"I found it!" he shouted into the phone, relief flooding his voice.

On the other end, Sarah exhaled audibly. "Thank God. Let's get this to the client ASAP."

Hours later, after the file had been delivered and the immediate crisis had been averted, Michael leaned back in his chair. The office buzzed with the usual energy, but he felt strangely detached from it all. It was clear now: the way he had been running his business wasn't just inefficient—it was reckless. He was one misplaced file away from disaster, and the worst part? He had known it all along.

Michael picked up *Order in Chaos* again, flipping to the next chapter. He couldn't ignore it any longer: he needed help.

Chapter 4: An Unexpected Ally

Michael Davis sat at his desk, the faint glow of his computer screen reflecting in his tired eyes. He had spent hours clearing out old files, reorganizing his emails, and meticulously setting up priority lists based on the techniques from Oliver's book. It felt good, productive even, but there was still a gnawing sense of impending doom as the weight of his disorganized business bore down on him. The inbox zero method had worked, his desk was immaculate, but no matter how clean everything looked, the chaos behind the scenes was undeniable.

Davis & Co. was still a ticking time bomb, and with every tick, Michael felt the pressure mounting. The staff was stretched thin, clients were growing impatient, and the looming deadline for their biggest project yet—the Davis & Co. system overhaul—was less than two weeks away. He could almost feel the walls closing in, and his to-do list seemed to multiply each time he glanced at it.

He sighed and leaned back in his chair, rubbing his temples. He was determined not to revert to his old ways—reacting rather than planning, micromanaging instead of delegating. He had been through that cycle too many times, and this time had to be different.

Knock, knock.

The sound jarred him from his thoughts. Michael blinked, realizing he had zoned out entirely. He didn't get many interruptions—most of his team knew to leave him alone when he was in the thick of work.

"Come in," he called, straightening up.

The door creaked open, and Alex, the quiet junior developer, poked his head in. Of all the employees, Alex was the last person Michael had expected to see. The guy was a bit of a mystery—introverted, kept his head down, and didn't mingle much with the rest of the team. But he was good at his job. Reliable. Which, in these days, was a rare commodity.

"Hey, Michael," Alex said, his voice soft but steady. He stepped inside, a small tablet clutched in his hand. "I, um, I heard about the Davis & Co. project. And... I wanted to offer my help."

Michael raised an eyebrow, caught off guard by the offer. "Your help?"

Alex nodded. "Yeah, I've worked on similar systems before, and I've got a few ideas on how we could streamline things. I think it would save us a lot of time."

For a moment, Michael was silent, processing what was happening. He had been so fixated on shouldering the burden himself that he hadn't even considered asking for help. It was his business, his responsibility. But the project was spiraling out of control, and perhaps this was the break he hadn't seen coming.

"You'd be willing to take that on?" Michael asked, his tone a mixture of hope and skepticism.

Alex gave a small smile, a flicker of confidence shining through his usually reserved demeanor. "Of course. We're all part of the same team, right?"

Michael found himself nodding, a wave of unexpected relief washing over him. "Yeah. We are."

Over the next few days, Alex proved himself to be much more than just a quiet junior developer. He didn't just assist with the Davis & Co. project; he took the lead on certain aspects, introducing a new project management system that blew Michael's mind. It wasn't just a tweak here or a shortcut there—Alex had a vision. He streamlined communication between team members, created a centralized hub for all the tasks, and broke down the complex project into manageable steps that the entire team could follow.

Michael watched in awe as the transformation took place. The team's productivity skyrocketed. Where there had once been confusion and miscommunication, there was now clarity and efficiency. The once-dreaded deadlines didn't seem so impossible anymore. Michael even found himself delegating more tasks, trusting Alex to take care of the technical side while he focused on strategy. For the first time in months, he felt like he was regaining control.

But just as the tide was turning, a new problem emerged.

One morning, as Michael sipped his coffee and scrolled through his emails, a message from Davis & Co. appeared in his inbox with an ominous subject line: **Urgent: Legal Matter**. His heart sank. He clicked it open, his stomach churning as he read the terse lines.

Dear Mr. Davis,

We regret to inform you that due to recent developments, we must temporarily halt all work on the project. A legal issue has arisen involving your company's handling of sensitive data, and we require immediate action before any further collaboration can proceed.

Michael's mind raced. Legal issue? What data? He had no idea what they were talking about.

His phone buzzed on the desk, a call coming through from his attorney, Linda Grayson. With a shaking hand, he answered, barely able to get out a greeting before Linda launched into the news.

"Michael, you're in trouble," she said bluntly. "It looks like someone in your company made a critical error in data compliance. The client's security protocols were breached, and now they're questioning your entire operation. If you don't fix this, they could sue for breach of contract."

Michael felt the blood drain from his face. "What... What are you talking about? I've been watching this project closely."

"It wasn't you, Michael," Linda said. "It was someone on your team. You need to get ahead of this, fast. Or this could sink the entire deal."

As soon as the call ended, Michael paced the room, his thoughts racing. Who could have made such a massive mistake? His mind immediately flashed to Alex, the new star of the team, who had recently taken control of the project. Could it have been him?

His gut twisted with uncertainty. He had put so much trust in Alex, but now, doubt crept in. There was only one way to find out.

Michael stormed down the hallway and straight to Alex's office. The door was slightly ajar, and he could see Alex hunched over his desk, furiously typing away. Michael knocked hard, startling him.

"Alex, we need to talk," Michael said, his voice tighter than he intended.

Alex looked up, surprised but calm. "What's going on?"

Michael handed him the email from Davis & Co., watching closely for any sign of guilt. Alex's eyes scanned the screen, his face remaining neutral.

"I didn't do this," Alex said firmly, pushing the laptop away. "I know the systems we've been working on. There's no way I would have made a mistake like that."

Michael searched his face, looking for any crack in his resolve, but Alex remained steady. "Then who did?" Michael asked, his voice low.

Alex's brow furrowed as he thought for a moment. "It could be someone on the data migration team. I haven't been directly involved with that. But I can help you figure this out."

Michael hesitated, his emotions swirling. He had been so quick to suspect Alex, but maybe he had been wrong. Maybe Alex really was the ally he needed, not the source of his problems.

With a deep breath, Michael made his decision. "Alright, let's figure this out together."

But little did Michael know, the real culprit was closer than he realized, and this was just the beginning of a much deeper unraveling.

Chapter 5: The Brink of Disaster

Michael Davis sat in his dimly lit office, savoring the rare moment of quiet that signaled the end of another long day. For the first time in what felt like months, he allowed himself to breathe, basking in a fleeting sense of control. The chaos of the past few years—expanding his consulting firm, juggling client demands, and managing internal politics—seemed to have calmed, if only for a moment. He leaned back in his chair, closing his eyes, letting the tension in his shoulders melt away.

But peace, like everything in Michael's world, was temporary.

A sharp knock on the door shattered the stillness. His assistant, Claire, stepped inside, her face strained as she handed him a thick, official-looking envelope.

"It just arrived," she said quietly, her eyes betraying a mixture of sympathy and unease.

Michael's stomach clenched as he took the envelope. The return address, cold and unforgiving, read: **Internal Revenue Service.**

His heart raced. **IRS? Why now?**

For a moment, Michael debated leaving the letter unopened, but he knew better. Slowly, deliberately, he tore the seal and unfolded the letter. The words *"Your business is under audit"* leaped off the page like a death sentence.

Years of poor bookkeeping, half-hearted attempts at organizing receipts, and missed tax filings crashed into his mind. He had always known it might catch up to him, but like many entrepreneurs, he had chosen to push the problem to the back burner, hoping it would magically resolve itself. Now, it was too late.

Michael let the letter slip from his fingers, feeling the weight of it pull him down as if it were an anchor. The office, once a place of control, now felt suffocating. He stared at the ceiling, a wave of helplessness washing over him.

For the first time in a long time, he felt paralyzed.

The next morning, Michael drove aimlessly before ending up in front of *The Tidy Mind,* the modest office of Oliver Grant, his business coach and confidant. He didn't have an appointment, but that didn't matter. Oliver had always been there for him during moments of crisis.

Oliver glanced up from his desk as Michael walked in, eyes hollow, jaw set in frustration.

"What's wrong, Michael?" Oliver asked, his voice calm but probing.

Michael sighed heavily and handed him the letter.

Oliver read it, his face revealing no hint of surprise. "I see," he said after a moment, handing the letter back. "You're under audit."

"I don't even know where to begin," Michael muttered, dropping into the chair across from Oliver's desk. "If this audit goes south, we're talking thousands—no, hundreds of thousands—in fines. The company could fold."

Oliver leaned back, interlocking his fingers behind his head. "Michael, you've faced impossible situations before. Remember the Turner contract? Everyone said it was dead, but you pulled through."

"This isn't the same," Michael interrupted, shaking his head. "The IRS... this is different. They don't negotiate. They just take."

Oliver remained unshaken. "It *is* the same, Michael. You're overwhelmed by the size of the problem, not the problem itself. The key is to break it down into parts. One piece at a time."

Michael exhaled, his gaze falling to the floor. "It feels like I'm drowning in it. Years of bad decisions..."

"I know," Oliver said, his voice steady. "But you don't need to solve this overnight. Right now, the goal is to get a handle on things. Start with the basics—organize your records, figure out where the real issues are, and build from there."

The advice was simple, but it felt like a lifeline. Michael left Oliver's office with a small flicker of hope, but the mountain ahead still loomed large.

Back in the office that night, Michael sat at his desk, surrounded by mountains of papers, invoices, and financial statements. His vision blurred as he tried to make sense of the mess. His phone buzzed—it was Alex, his head of operations and one of the few people he truly trusted.

"Hey, I heard what's going on. You need help?" Alex asked.

Michael hesitated for a moment, then nodded to himself. "Yeah. I need you to pull every financial record we have—accounts, invoices, anything. We need to make sense of this chaos."

"I'm on it," Alex replied without hesitation. "I'll be there in 30 minutes."

True to his word, Alex arrived, laptop in hand, sleeves rolled up. The two men worked late into the night, meticulously combing through the past few years of financial transactions. Alex's technical expertise was invaluable—he managed to pull data from accounts Michael had forgotten about, organizing it all into something resembling order.

"This is a mess, but it's not unfixable," Alex said, glancing at Michael, who was rubbing his temples. "We just need to break it down, like Oliver said."

As the nights dragged on, sleepless and stressful, the pile of papers slowly shrank, replaced by spreadsheets and reports that began to make sense. For the first time in weeks, Michael saw a glimmer of hope.

The day of the audit arrived, and Michael sat in his office, waiting for the IRS agents. His mind raced through worst-case scenarios—his company shuttered, employees left without jobs, his reputation destroyed. He forced himself to take deep breaths, remembering Oliver's words: *One piece at a time.*

When the agents finally arrived, their demeanor was professional but cold. The audit process was brutal. Questions about missing receipts, unclear expenses, and unexplained financial discrepancies came fast and hard. Each question felt like a hammer strike, but Michael held his ground.

Alex had come prepared too, backing up every claim with organized data. The once-cluttered chaos of their financial records had been reduced to something manageable, something defendable.

After what felt like days of interrogation, the agents left. Michael sat in silence, the weight of uncertainty still pressing on him.

Weeks passed before the IRS delivered their verdict: there would be fines—steep ones—but nothing that would break the company. The audit was a narrow escape, but the business would survive.

Michael sat in his office that night, staring out the window. The city lights flickered in the distance, and for the first time in what seemed like forever, he exhaled.

He knew he'd dodged a bullet, but the close call left its mark. This wasn't just about an audit; it was a lesson. If he didn't take control of his business, chaos would eventually consume him. He had escaped this time, but would he be so lucky again?

The door to his office creaked open, and Claire poked her head in. "Everything okay, Michael?"

He nodded slowly. "Yeah... for now."

But deep down, he knew the battle wasn't over. It was only just beginning.

Chapter 6: Tipping Point

The relief from the audit victory barely settled before the storm clouds began to gather again. TechWave Solutions, Michael Davis's largest and most lucrative client, had discovered a glitch in their new software integration. A seemingly minor coding oversight snowballed into a systemic failure, causing delays across TechWave's global platform. The error wasn't just inconvenient; it threatened their customer base.

Michael received the call late at night. His phone vibrated on the bedside table; its glow harsh against the darkness of his bedroom. The CEO of TechWave, Dean Cross, was on the other end. His voice was icy, clinical—much like the way surgeons talk before they make the first incision.

"Michael," Dean began, without preamble, "we've got a serious problem. And we're not happy."

Michael's heart sank, his stomach turning cold. He had faced tense moments before, but the steel in Dean's tone was different. It wasn't frustration—it was the edge of a blade ready to cut through the contract they had built together over years of collaboration.

"What exactly is the issue?" Michael asked, trying to keep his voice steady.

"There's been a massive disruption with the integration. Clients in Europe are pulling back from their deployments. The glitch on your end caused a cascade failure in our system, and we're hemorrhaging clients. I've got my board breathing down my neck. If this isn't resolved by Friday, we're done, Michael. Consider this your official notice."

Michael sat up in bed, a cold sweat forming on his brow. "Friday? Dean, that's—"

"Impossible? Maybe. But it's the only option. Fix it, or TechWave moves on. And we'll make sure every potential partner you have knows why." Dean hung up, leaving Michael in stunned silence.

He sat there, staring at the screen as his phone's glow faded, the weight of his company's future suddenly heavier than ever. **This is it**, he thought, staring at the ceiling, his mind racing. **If we lose TechWave, NextGen might not recover.**

But this time, Michael refused to let fear grip him the way it had during the audit. Failure wasn't an option, but neither was panic. He could feel it in his bones—this was a pivotal moment, the kind where leaders are made or broken.

The next morning, Michael gathered his top executives and team leads in the conference room. There was a tension in the air that everyone felt as they filed in, their faces drawn and tired from late-night troubleshooting. The stakes were clear; the weight of TechWave's potential departure hung like an executioner's blade.

As soon as everyone settled, Michael took a deep breath and began.

"Look," he said, standing at the head of the table, his eyes scanning the room. "We've faced bigger challenges before. This deadline is tight—hell, it's more than tight. But we can meet it. We've got 48 hours to fix this, and I know we can. I've seen what you all are capable of, and I trust you to come through. So, here's the plan."

He turned to the whiteboard, scribbling furiously as he broke the massive problem down into tasks, each team responsible for one critical piece of the solution.

"We stay focused on what we can control. No distractions. No second-guessing. We fix this."

The room was quiet, the gravity of the situation sinking in. But there was also a spark in the eyes of his team, a sense of determination that hadn't been there before. It was like Michael had given them permission to be confident in the face of chaos.

Julia, the lead software architect, leaned forward, her pen tapping against her notebook. "We can rework the faulty integration, but we'll need to pull in extra hands from the design team. We're talking round-the-clock coding."

"I don't care if we have to bring in the janitorial staff to help," Michael said with a wry smile, trying to inject some levity. "We're going to make this happen."

The next 48 hours were a blur of coffee cups, bleary eyes, and furious typing. The office hummed with an energy that oscillated between desperation and determination. Michael barely left his desk, constantly coordinating between teams, checking on progress, and calming tempers as tensions inevitably flared.

At 3 a.m. on the second night, Julia stormed into Michael's office, looking exhausted but animated. "We've found the root cause," she said, out of breath. "It's in the legacy code. We can patch it, but it's going to take time."

"How much time?" Michael asked, his heart pounding.

"Five hours. Maybe six, if nothing else breaks. But if we can pull it off..."

Michael didn't let her finish. He was already up, moving towards the war room where the rest of the team was gathered. "Everyone, listen up! We've got a clear path to fixing this. Julia's found the issue, and we're deploying in five hours."

He saw the looks on their faces—exhaustion mixed with a faint glimmer of hope. They had been through the wringer, and now, it was time to push through the final stretch.

The clock seemed to tick faster as they worked. Each minute was a reminder of the looming deadline, a countdown to what could either be salvation or disaster. Michael didn't allow himself to think about the "what ifs." He was in survival mode, laser-focused on the task at hand.

Friday morning arrived, and so did TechWave's board meeting. Dean Cross was waiting for an update, and Michael knew they had no more chances left. At 9:58 a.m., just minutes before the hard deadline, the team pushed the final updates live. The office was so quiet you could hear the hum of the servers.

"Is it holding?" someone asked, breaking the silence.

Julia refreshed the screen, her eyes scanning for any signs of failure. The room held its collective breath. Finally, she smiled.

"It's holding."

A cheer erupted, but Michael barely heard it. He was already reaching for his phone, dialing Dean.

"Michael," Dean said as he picked up. There was a pause. "I'm seeing the reports come in. It looks good."

Michael exhaled, feeling the tension drain from his body.

"You pulled it off," Dean continued. "I'll be honest—I didn't think you would. But you did. And because of that, we're not only keeping our contract, we're expanding it."

Michael stood there, stunned. He thanked Dean and hung up, his mind still reeling from the rollercoaster of the last two days. He had done it. They had done it.

But just as Michael felt the relief wash over him, his phone buzzed again. This time, it was an unknown number. Curious, he picked it up.

"Mr. Davis?" The voice on the other end was formal but unfamiliar. "This is Sandra Jenkins from the Federal Trade Commission. We need to speak with you regarding an ongoing investigation into one of your vendors."

Michael's heart skipped a beat. He had just pulled off one impossible save. Now, another crisis loomed, and this one felt even more dangerous.

Life had thrown him another curveball—one that could unravel everything he had just fought to hold together.

Chapter 7: A Betrayal Unfolds

Michael Davis had barely settled into the sweet taste of victory after closing the deal with TechWave when the unthinkable happened. The early morning light streamed through his office window as he sipped his coffee, his mind already pivoting to the next big project. He casually opened his laptop to catch up on emails, but his relaxed expression quickly tightened as he scrolled through his inbox. There it was—a single subject line that shattered his focus: **"Client Transfer Notification."**

The email was short and cold, its tone devoid of the warmth Michael had come to expect from his clients. It was from Horizon Dynamics, one of NextGen Strategies' most lucrative accounts, informing him of their decision to transfer their business to a new firm. His brow furrowed as he read the name of the new company—**Phoenix Consultancy**.

A knot formed in his stomach. Phoenix Consultancy. He hadn't heard of it before. He quickly Googled the name, and his breath caught in his throat. The website was polished but simple, a typical startup's site. The owner, however, was no stranger. There, on the "About Us" page, was a professional headshot of none other than **Sarah Jensen**, his former project manager. She smiled confidently at the camera, her bio extolling her years of experience in strategic consulting. Experience she had gained working directly under Michael's guidance.

Sarah had been a rising star at NextGen, always two steps ahead of everyone else. Her departure six months earlier had seemed abrupt, though she had left on good terms—or so he thought. Michael's hand trembled as he scrolled through the list of clients on Phoenix Consultancy's portfolio. His heart sank. Horizon Dynamics wasn't the only name he recognized.

Global Innovators.

Synergetic Solutions.

QuantumTech Ventures.

She had poached several of NextGen's biggest accounts.

The phone slipped from his hand and hit the desk with a dull thud. He sat back, staring at the screen in disbelief. His pulse quickened, and for a moment, he felt like the room was closing in around him. Years of hard work, years of building relationships, carefully navigating contracts and partnerships—all of it was unraveling before his eyes.

"How could I have been so blind?" Michael muttered under his breath, but the words felt heavier than he'd anticipated. He grabbed his phone and dialed Alex, his operations manager and one of the few people he still trusted at the company.

"Alex, I need you in my office now."

Fifteen minutes later, Alex strode in, his usual calm demeanor punctuated by the tension in his jawline as he sensed the urgency in Michael's voice. Michael waved him over without looking up, still fixated on his screen.

"Look at this," Michael said, turning his laptop towards Alex.

Alex squinted at the email and then the webpage. His face darkened. "Sarah? What the hell is this?"

"She's started her own firm," Michael said, his voice bitter. "And she's taken our top clients with her."

Alex's eyes widened, but then his expression hardened. "That's... this is ruthless," he muttered, running a hand through his hair. "She always had ambition, but this? What are you going to do?"

"I don't know yet," Michael admitted, his voice cracking. "If more clients follow, we're screwed. NextGen won't survive this."

They sat in silence for a moment, the weight of the situation sinking in. Michael knew the stakes. If Sarah kept this up, not only would NextGen's revenue plummet, but its reputation would be tarnished beyond repair. Trust in his leadership, both from clients and within his own team, would evaporate.

Michael reached for his phone again and called Oliver, his head of legal, desperate for advice on how to handle the situation. The phone rang once. Twice. Voicemail. Michael cursed under his breath.

"We need a plan," Alex said, his voice steady but serious. "If we don't act now, she's going to strip everything we've built."

Michael stared at the screen, his mind a blur of strategies that all felt too little, too late. His thoughts were interrupted by another notification—a new email. This one was from **Synergetic Solutions**. His heart sank further. Another client gone.

His mind spiraled. How had he missed the warning signs? He recalled how Sarah had been asking more questions about client contracts in her last months at the company. She'd started attending meetings she had no need to attend, gathering information from all corners of NextGen. He'd chalked it up to her ambition. Now he realized it had been something more sinister.

"She's smart," Michael said, a hollow laugh escaping his lips. "She waited until the TechWave deal was finalized before making her move. Now we're stretched thin."

Alex frowned. "She timed this. Knew you'd be too focused on the big win to notice her setting up shop."

Michael's eyes darkened. The betrayal wasn't just professional—it was deeply personal. He had trusted Sarah, mentored her, even confided in her about his vision for the future of NextGen. And now, here she was, not only undermining him but stealing the foundation of everything he had built.

Suddenly, his phone rang, startling him from his thoughts. It was Oliver.

"Michael, I'm sorry I missed your call. What's going on?" Oliver's voice was brisk but attentive.

Michael filled him in on the situation, outlining the clients that had jumped ship and Sarah's role in all of it.

Oliver's silence on the other end was unnerving.

"Listen, this isn't just a business problem, Michael. It sounds like Sarah might have breached her non-compete agreement. If we can prove that she poached clients while still under contract, we could have a case."

Michael's grip on the phone tightened. "What are our chances?"

"I'll need to dig into her contract and start gathering evidence. But Michael," Oliver hesitated, "this is going to get ugly. Public lawsuits can damage your reputation just as much as losing these clients."

Michael closed his eyes. It was a catch-22. Fight back, and he risked dragging NextGen through a public legal battle. Let it slide, and Sarah would continue siphoning off clients until there was nothing left to save.

"I need time to think," Michael said finally, his voice taut.

"Don't wait too long," Oliver warned. "Every day that passes, she gets stronger."

As the call ended, Michael turned back to Alex. "We need to hit back, but smartly. I don't want to rush into this without a solid strategy."

Alex nodded, a grim expression on his face. "I'll start pulling together a list of our key clients, the ones we can't afford to lose. We need to shore up their loyalty, make sure they're not tempted by whatever Sarah's offering."

Michael looked out the window, his mind already calculating his next move. The betrayal was brutal, but it wasn't the end. He wouldn't let it be.

But deep down, he knew this was only the beginning.

Chapter 8: The Guide's Disappearance

The sun was dipping low as Michael hurried through the city streets, his heart pounding in rhythm with each frantic step. The chaos at the office had reached a tipping point, and Michael's nerves were unraveling. The memory of Oliver's serene voice had been his anchor, guiding him through moments where he felt lost in the storm of decisions, deadlines, and the growing abyss of failure looming in the distance. Today, more than ever, he needed the man's steady advice. He turned the corner onto the street where The Tidy Mind was tucked away, the old bookstore that had become a refuge for him.

But something was wrong.

Michael stopped in his tracks, blinking as if his eyes were playing tricks on him. The quaint, familiar building was gone. Not boarded up, not locked with a 'Closed' sign hanging in the window—it was gone. An empty lot stood in its place, weeds poking through the cracks in the sidewalk where the bookstore's stoop used to be. His heart, already racing, skipped a beat.

"What the...?" he muttered, stepping forward as if the building might reappear if he got close enough.

He spun around, searching for anyone who might explain the bizarre scene. His eyes landed on an older woman passing by with her groceries. "Excuse me," Michael blurted out, his voice shaking with urgency. "There was a bookstore here, The Tidy Mind? It's been here for years...you know it, right?"

The woman raised an eyebrow, casting a glance over her shoulder at the vacant lot. "Bookstore?" She shook her head, confused. "I've lived in this neighborhood for over thirty years. There's never been a bookstore here, young man. I think you've got the wrong place."

"No, I'm sure of it," Michael insisted, but the woman was already walking away, shaking her head.

He felt a cold shiver ripple up his spine. His hands started trembling. He rushed toward the coffee shop on the corner, desperate for any confirmation. Inside, he spotted a barista he'd spoken to a few times when grabbing coffee before visiting Oliver.

"Hey," Michael said, approaching the counter with wild eyes. "The bookstore down the street—The Tidy Mind. Where did it go?"

The barista looked at him blankly. "I don't know what you're talking about, man. There's never been a bookstore there."

Michael's heart sank further. He stumbled outside, staring at the spot where the bookstore had once stood, his mind reeling. Was it possible that Oliver—his guide, the man who had given him the clarity he desperately needed in the middle of his business chaos—wasn't real? No, that couldn't be. He remembered the countless conversations, the sage advice, the cryptic but calming presence of Oliver. It had been too real.

Hadn't it?

Michael's phone buzzed in his pocket, jolting him out of his spiral. He glanced down at the screen: 5 missed calls from his business partner, Sarah. He swiped the notifications away. He wasn't ready to deal with the collapse of his business right now. He needed to figure out what had happened to Oliver, to The Tidy Mind. None of this made sense.

Forcing himself to focus, he began to think logically. Maybe Oliver had moved, or maybe the shop was closed temporarily for renovations. That had to be it. But no one even seemed to know it existed.

Desperate for answers, Michael pulled out his phone and began frantically searching for anything about The Tidy Mind—its address, its business registration, its owner. But every search came up blank, as if the store had never existed. Panic clawed at him as he scrolled through old emails, texts—any correspondence with Oliver. Nothing. Not a single digital trace.

He started to feel light-headed, his legs weak beneath him. Was this all in his head? Had the stress of the business—the mounting debts, the sleepless nights—finally broken him? But that couldn't be. He *remembered* Oliver. He *remembered* the books, the dust on the shelves, the warm smell of old pages, the tea Oliver always brewed in that old ceramic pot.

Suddenly, Michael's phone buzzed again. A message from an unknown number flashed on the screen:

"You're closer to the truth than you think."

His heart stopped. He stared at the words, blinking in disbelief. Was it Oliver? Before he could respond, another message appeared:

"Follow the chaos. Trust yourself."

What did that mean? Trust himself? Michael had been doing anything but that lately. The only reason he had made any progress was because of Oliver's advice. Or was that the point? Had Oliver merely been a figment of his subconscious, guiding him through what he already knew but was too afraid to admit?

The more Michael thought about it, the more things didn't add up. He never knew much about Oliver—where he lived, his background, how he had come to own a bookstore that no one seemed to know existed. Everything had seemed too convenient, too perfectly timed.

Michael sat down on the curb, his head in his hands, staring at the empty lot in front of him. Without Oliver, he was alone, thrust back into the swirling chaos of his life and business, where nothing made sense anymore.

The phone buzzed one last time:

"The answers you seek are already within you. Look inside."

And then, nothing. No more messages. No more Oliver. Just the silence of an empty street and a vacant lot where a store—where *his* guide—had once been.

Michael stood up slowly, staring at the barren space, feeling a strange calm wash over him. Maybe the store had never existed. Maybe Oliver wasn't real, or maybe he was. Either way, Michael realized with a quiet certainty that he couldn't depend on a guide anymore. He couldn't keep running to someone else to fix the mess his life had become.

The answers were within him. Oliver—or whoever had sent those messages—was right. The chaos was still there, but Michael wasn't as lost in it as he had thought.

He pocketed his phone and took one last glance at the lot before walking away. For the first time in a long while, Michael felt something stirring inside him—a sense of direction, not from someone else, but from himself.

And for the first time, he wasn't afraid of facing the chaos on his own.

Chapter 9: The Spiral

Without Oliver's support, Michael's grip on his business unraveled faster than he could have imagined. What had once seemed like small fires, easily extinguished with strategic moves and late-night work sessions, were now growing into uncontrollable blazes. The fallout from Sarah's betrayal was still reverberating through his company, making every decision feel like a gamble he was doomed to lose.

Michael sat in his office, staring at the mountain of paperwork that seemed to reproduce on its own. Every financial report, every client email, every missed deadline felt like a personal failure. The weight was suffocating. Despite Alex's relentless drive to pick up the pieces, they were both drowning.

"Maybe it's time to pivot, look for new markets," Alex said one afternoon, the bags under his eyes showing just how hard he'd been working. "We can't keep losing clients like this and expect to survive."

Michael ran his hand through his hair, sighing deeply. "And pivot to what, Alex? Every time we turn, there's a wall waiting to stop us."

Alex's optimism had always been Michael's buoy, but even now, he seemed to be floundering. "We have to do *something*."

The silence that followed was heavy with unspoken truths. They both knew the situation was critical. Michael had lost something far more damaging than clients—he had lost confidence. And worse, he couldn't shake the feeling that this spiral was something he had created.

That evening, Michael arrived home well past dinner, the house quiet save for the faint hum of the refrigerator. Jenny was waiting for him, arms crossed, her eyes hard with the frustration she had kept bottled for weeks.

"You're disappearing again," she said, her voice cracking at the edges. "I thought things were getting better. You were here. With us. Now you're back to being... a ghost. And we can't keep doing this."

Michael didn't have the strength to argue. His heart was heavy, his mind was numb, and the weariness seeped into his bones. He had nothing left to give.

"I'm trying, Jenny," he whispered, though the words felt hollow even to him. He wasn't trying. Not really. He was surviving.

"No," she shot back, "you're not trying, Michael. You're running. From me, from the kids, from this mess. And one day you'll wake up and we won't be here anymore." She paused, her lips quivering. "I can't watch you destroy yourself. Not again."

Her words stung like salt on an open wound, but he knew she was right. He *was* disappearing, and this time, the fear and chaos were winning.

For the next few days, Michael buried himself in work, spending more time at the office than ever before. But no matter how hard he worked, the cracks were growing. Every client call brought more bad news—another defection, another missed opportunity. The client roster, once a symbol of success, was thinning rapidly. Each loss was like another thread in the unraveling of his world.

One late night, while scrolling through an endless series of emails, Michael noticed something peculiar. A message from an unknown sender. The subject line simply read: *You're not seeing the whole picture.*

His heart skipped a beat as he clicked it open. The email contained nothing but a cryptic line: *You think the spiral ends here, but it doesn't. Call me.* Below was a phone number he didn't recognize.

At first, Michael dismissed it as spam, but something about the timing gnawed at him. Was it a prank? A competitor? Or something else entirely? Unable to resist, he dialed the number, half-expecting no one to answer.

The line clicked, and a woman's voice came through, calm and authoritative. "I wondered how long it would take for you to call."

"Who is this?" Michael asked, feeling a knot form in his stomach.

"You know who I am," she replied coolly. "I've been watching your business for some time now. You're in over your head, but there's a way out. You've been playing the wrong game, Michael."

His throat tightened. "I don't know what you're talking about."

"Sarah didn't betray you," she said, cutting through his denial. "She was just the beginning. You're being played, and you don't even know it."

Michael's pulse quickened. "Who's behind this?"

"All in due time. Meet me tomorrow at The Red Lantern, 3 p.m. sharp. I'll explain everything."

Before he could respond, the line went dead.

The next morning, he woke with an unfamiliar sense of urgency. He debated telling Alex about the call but decided against it. This felt personal—too personal to involve anyone else. The Red Lantern was an old, run-down bar on the outskirts of the city, the kind of place where secrets felt safe. He arrived early, scanning the room for the mysterious woman.

A few minutes later, she entered—tall, poised, and dressed in business attire that was far too sharp for the setting. She sat down across from him without a word.

"I don't have a lot of time," she began. "But I'll tell you this—there are forces at play you can't see. Oliver leaving wasn't an accident. Sarah wasn't just after your clients. There's a group targeting businesses like yours, exploiting their vulnerabilities, and tearing them apart from the inside."

Michael leaned forward, his mind reeling. "Who are they?"

"I can't say more right now, but you need to protect what's left. Trust no one." She slid a business card across the table. "When you're ready to hear the rest, call me."

Michael looked down at the card. No name, no title. Just a single word: *Solve.*

By the time he looked up, she was gone.

Back at the office, Michael's paranoia grew. He couldn't focus. Every conversation, every deal, every employee interaction felt like a potential trap. Who could he trust? He wanted to confide in Alex, but the seed of doubt had already been planted. How deep did this go?

Suddenly, an email alert pinged on his laptop. It was from Alex: *Urgent meeting in 10 minutes. Something's wrong.*

Michael's heart pounded as he opened the email. Was this the setup? Was Alex part of it?

He felt the spiral pulling him deeper. And for the first time, Michael didn't know how to claw his way out.

Chapter 10: Secrets from the Past

Michael sat at his desk, the familiar chaos of papers, invoices, and contracts strewn around him, reflecting the turbulence in his own mind. He had thought things couldn't get worse. His business was teetering on the brink of collapse, investors were backing out, and key employees had started looking elsewhere. But as he dug through old files, hoping to find some overlooked opportunity, he made a discovery that shifted everything.

It was hidden in plain sight, tucked inside a dusty, dog-eared book he had almost forgotten about—**Order in Chaos**, the same one Oliver had given him as a gift after their first meeting. A cryptic gesture at the time, Michael had brushed it off as one of Oliver's quirks. But now, as the book fell open, something unusual slipped out. A set of old, yellowing notes, written in hurried, fragmented handwriting.

He skimmed over the scribbled lines—thoughts too erratic to make sense at first. Sentences that seemed incomplete, jotted down as if someone was in a rush. But one line, buried among the disjointed words, stopped him cold.

"You will find the answers you seek in your past."

Michael sat back, staring at the page. It sounded like one of Oliver's many cryptic pieces of advice, the ones that often seemed meaningless until they made perfect sense. At first, he dismissed it as just another puzzle from his elusive mentor. But something about the words felt different, weightier. He flipped through more of the pages, scanning for clues. What he found wasn't just musings on chaos and order but hints—tiny breadcrumbs—that suggested a deeper connection between Oliver and Michael's life than he had ever imagined.

Something stirred in Michael's memory, a vague recollection of his father speaking of a business partner from decades ago, someone who had vanished from their lives after a devastating failure. His father had never mentioned the man's name in detail—only that they had been close, that their shared vision had fallen apart, and that it had changed everything for their family.

Determined to understand the mystery, Michael dove into research. He combed through public records, old newspaper clippings, and archives. The more he dug, the more unnerved he became. After hours of searching, a name surfaced: **Oliver Gray**, his father's old partner, the man who had co-founded their ill-fated venture. It was the same Oliver who had appeared in Michael's life just months earlier, seemingly out of nowhere, offering to guide him through his own business turmoil.

Michael's breath hitched. How long had Oliver known? Had he approached Michael deliberately, with full knowledge of their shared history, or was this some cosmic coincidence?

The weight of it all pressed down on him. He needed answers, and there was only one man who could provide them.

That evening, Michael called Oliver, his heart racing as the phone rang.

"Michael," Oliver's calm voice answered. "What's on your mind?"

There was a pause, heavy with unspoken words. "I found something," Michael began, trying to keep his voice steady. "In the book you gave me. Notes. And I did some research. Oliver, why didn't you tell me you knew my father?"

For the first time since they had met, Michael detected a crack in Oliver's cool demeanor. The silence on the other end of the line was palpable, and when Oliver spoke again, his voice had lost its usual ease.

"I was going to tell you, Michael. But not like this."

"Like what? How could you not tell me? You were his partner!" Michael's voice rose, the anger barely contained. "Did you come into my life because of him? Is this all about some unfinished business between you two?"

Oliver sighed. "It's not that simple. Yes, I knew your father. We were partners. But this isn't about the past—it's about you. I saw the same potential in you that I saw in him, and I didn't want you to make the same mistakes."

"And yet, here I am. Facing failure just like he did." Michael's voice cracked with bitterness. "You think this is some kind of redemption for you? Helping me fix the mess you both left behind?"

"It's not about redemption," Oliver said, his voice firmer now. "It's about giving you the chance to break the cycle."

Michael's mind was reeling, the pieces of the puzzle finally snapping into place. This wasn't just about saving his business. It was about something deeper—escaping a legacy of failure that had haunted his family for years.

"How much of this did you plan, Oliver? Did you seek me out because you felt guilty for what happened to my father?"

"I sought you out because I knew you were strong enough to break free of the past," Oliver said quietly. "Your father... he was brilliant, but he couldn't see the forest for the trees. He chased perfection, control, and when it all came crashing down, he couldn't recover. I've been watching you, and I see the same drive in you—but also the same blind spots."

Michael stood, pacing his office as the words sank in. The anger he had felt moments before gave way to confusion. He wasn't sure whether to be furious or grateful, to trust Oliver or to cut him out of his life completely.

"I don't know if I can trust you," Michael said finally. "How do I know you're not just here to fix your own mistakes? To play puppet master in my life like you did with my father?"

Oliver's tone softened, but there was an urgency to his words. "Trust isn't given—it's earned, and I know I've given you every reason to doubt me. But I also know that you're on the verge of something great, Michael. Something that can change not only your life but the legacy of your family. The choice is yours whether you want my help. But know this—I'm not here to control you. I'm here to help you see the chaos for what it is and find the order within it."

The words hung in the air between them, charged with meaning. Michael didn't know what to believe anymore, but one thing was clear: this journey wasn't just about him or his business. It was about breaking free from the shadows of the past, from the mistakes of those who had come before him.

And, for the first time, he realized he might just have the power to do it.

Chapter 11: Triumph or Defeat

Michael stood outside the office door, his hand gripping the cold metal handle. The same door he had passed through countless times now felt heavier, as if it symbolized the weight of the choices that had led him here. Armed with a new understanding of what went wrong, he wasn't just returning to work—he was walking into battle, not against his employees, not even against his competitors, but against himself.

The company was still standing, but just barely. The lines between personal and professional chaos had blurred so much that Michael could no longer tell where one ended and the other began. He took a deep breath and pushed the door open, stepping inside the place that had once been the embodiment of his ambition but had turned into a reflection of his deepest fears.

Jenny was right. His obsession with growth had almost destroyed everything that mattered. He knew it wasn't just the business that needed restructuring; his life did, too. His eyes fell on the photograph of their family at the beach, tucked away on a dusty shelf. Michael picked it up, wiping away the dust with his sleeve, and set it prominently on his desk.

"Not just the business," he whispered to himself. "Everything."

He walked down the hallway to his office, determined, but the voices of self-doubt still whispered in the background. Could he really fix this? Could he salvage the mess he had made, or was this just the final desperate grasp of a man already defeated?

The First Step

The first person he had to face wasn't Sarah, but Jenny. The tension at home had reached a breaking point, and he had allowed the cracks in his personal life to bleed into the office. He took a seat at his desk, opened his laptop, and typed an email—short, honest, raw. No business jargon, no excuses.

"Jenny, I'm sorry. Not just for neglecting you and the kids, but for letting work consume me to the point where I forgot why I was doing it all in the first place. I promise you, I'm setting boundaries from now on. Family comes first. We'll get through this. Please give me another chance."

He clicked 'send' and stared at the screen for a long time, unsure of what response to expect. But that was a bridge he'd cross when it came. For now, he had a business to face.

The Confrontation with Sarah

Michael knew that confronting Sarah was inevitable. Her betrayal had been a brutal wake-up call, but the truth was, the cracks in their professional relationship had been forming long before she walked out the door with half his clients. Michael hadn't just lost control of his business—he had lost control of his team, his people.

"Sarah," he called her the next morning. The phone rang longer than he expected before she picked up.

"Michael," her voice was icy, distant. She clearly wasn't expecting this call.

"I don't want to fight. We need to talk."

"About what? You've made it clear where you stand."

Michael paused, choosing his words carefully. "You're right. I made mistakes. I let things spiral, and I didn't see how it affected you and the rest of the team. I know you feel like I wasn't paying attention, but I was drowning, Sarah. I didn't know how to fix it, and I'm sorry you got caught in that mess."

Silence.

Then, after what felt like an eternity, she sighed. "Michael, you let it all fall apart. I tried to tell you. So did the others. You didn't listen."

"I know." Michael's voice was steady. "But I'm listening now. The clients you took—they're not just numbers to me anymore. I've learned that. I want to rebuild. If you're open to it, I'd like to meet and talk about how we can work together again. Not as boss and employee, but as partners. I won't make the same mistakes twice."

There was a pause on the other end. "I'll think about it," Sarah finally said before the line went dead.

The Harder Battle

But Sarah wasn't the hardest battle. The greatest enemy was still the chaos within himself. His own mind, his fear of failure, his constant need for control—these were the real obstacles. The business had grown faster than he was prepared to manage, and his need to control every aspect of it had become his undoing.

In the weeks that followed, Michael attacked the chaos with ruthless precision. He tore apart old processes, hired a coach to guide him through leadership training, and reorganized his workflow. For the first time in years, he let go of tasks he used to micromanage, delegating to his team. They weren't just employees anymore—they were his partners in survival.

One afternoon, as Michael sat reviewing the latest client retention figures, Jenny walked into his office, unannounced. She placed a cup of coffee on his desk and took a seat across from him, saying nothing at first.

"Thank you for the email," she said after a long pause. "I can see you're trying. But I need more than promises, Michael. So do the kids."

"I know," Michael said, rubbing his temples. "I'm not asking for you to forgive me overnight. Just...let me show you that I can change. Give me time. We'll fix this."

"I hope you're right," she said quietly, standing up. "Because if this doesn't change soon, I won't be sticking around."

Her words cut deep, but they fueled him even more.

An Unexpected Twist

Things seemed to be on the mend—until a storm that no one saw coming hit.

Two months later, a client filed a lawsuit. It was a minor contractual dispute, something that could easily be resolved under normal circumstances, but it couldn't have come at a worse time. The client was one of those Sarah had taken with her, and now, they were dragging the company's name through the mud, accusing Michael of mismanagement and breach of agreement.

It was a calculated move—someone from the inside had to have tipped them off. It had Sarah's fingerprints all over it.

"She's trying to ruin me," Michael muttered to himself, pacing the office late at night.

He dialed Sarah's number again, this time with a different tone. She answered on the second ring.

"I see what you're doing," Michael said, anger bubbling under the surface. "Is this how you want it to end?"

"I don't know what you're talking about," Sarah replied, but there was a slight tremor in her voice.

"You had a part in this lawsuit, didn't you?" Michael pressed. "You couldn't just leave and let things be. You had to try to burn it all down."

"Michael, I told you I'd think about working things out with you. But maybe you haven't learned as much as you think you have."

The line went dead. Michael threw his phone across the room, his heart pounding. How had he been so blind? Sarah had never intended to rebuild trust. She had been planning this all along.

This was more than a setback. This was war.

Triumph or Defeat?

The next few weeks were a blur of legal meetings, damage control, and long, sleepless nights. Yet, in the middle of the storm, Michael found clarity. The chaos wasn't the end—it was part of the process. He had learned to adapt, to rebuild from the ruins. His fear of failure no longer paralyzed him—it fueled him.

As the lawsuit moved forward, something surprising happened. Former clients, seeing the transparency with which Michael handled the situation, began to return. Slowly but surely, the tide turned.

One evening, after a particularly grueling day, Jenny sent him a simple text: *I see the change. Keep going.*

For the first time in months, Michael allowed himself a small smile. Triumph or defeat wasn't about winning or losing the lawsuit. It was about mastering the chaos within.

Whatever came next, Michael knew one thing: this time, he was ready.

Chapter 12: Order Restored

———

Months later, Michael stood in his office, the space a testament to transformation. The chaotic piles of paperwork had vanished, replaced by neatly labeled folders. A subtle hum of productivity filled the room, from the soft tapping of keyboards to the occasional ring of phones. Even the air felt lighter, as though the invisible weight that had pressed down on him for so long had lifted. The business was thriving once again, and his marriage—once on the brink—was stronger than it had been in years. He felt proud, but something gnawed at him, a shadow from the past that refused to disappear completely.

His phone buzzed—a text from his wife, Claire:

"Dinner tonight at 7? Don't forget."

He smiled and replied: *"Wouldn't miss it."*

He wandered around his office, surveying the scene, letting his eyes drift to the neatly arranged shelves and immaculate desk. As he pulled open an old, dusty drawer, the contents surprised him—a relic from a different time, when chaos had reigned over his life and business. He hadn't opened the drawer in years. Inside, amid forgotten paperwork and old memos, was a small, worn book—**Order in Chaos.**

Michael stared at it for a moment, his heartbeat quickening. The memories came flooding back. The cryptic advice from Oliver, the strange man who had appeared just when everything had started spiraling out of control. Who was he? Was he even real? Sometimes, Michael questioned his own recollections of those dark days. But now, as he held the book in his hand, it felt all too real.

He flipped through the pages and stopped when he saw a handwritten note on the inside of the back cover. The familiar, slanted handwriting belonged to Oliver:

"Chaos will always return, but now you know how to face it. Trust yourself."

The words hit Michael hard, as if they were meant for him in this exact moment. He smiled to himself, though uncertainty bubbled beneath the surface. Whether Oliver had been real or not didn't matter anymore. What mattered was the lesson he had learned. Chaos was a constant in life, but it didn't have to control him.

Michael closed the book and set it on his desk. His phone rang—it was Jake, his head of operations.

"Michael, you need to see this," Jake's voice crackled through the phone, laced with urgency. "Something's off with the numbers. There's a discrepancy we can't explain."

Michael's stomach tightened. **Discrepancy** was not a word he wanted to hear. Not after everything he had done to restore order. "I'll be right there," he said, grabbing his jacket.

As he made his way to the operations floor, his mind raced. Had chaos returned so soon? Was this just another test, like Oliver had warned? He walked into the operations room where his team was already gathered around a large monitor, showing a spreadsheet of financials—something was definitely wrong.

Jake pointed to the screen, his face pale. "Look here, these payments—they don't match up. We're missing close to half a million dollars."

Michael felt his blood run cold. **Half a million?** How could that have slipped through? He had put systems in place to prevent this. He took a deep breath, forcing himself to stay calm. Panic wouldn't solve this. He had learned that the hard way.

"Let's retrace our steps," Michael said, his voice firm. "Who's been handling these transactions?"

Jake hesitated. "That's the thing... it's coming from Oliver's old department."

Michael's heart skipped a beat. **Oliver?** The name alone felt like a ghost from the past, stirring up questions he thought he had left behind. But Oliver had been gone for months, hadn't he? Or had he ever really been here at all?

He pulled out his phone and checked the last correspondence he had with Oliver. There was nothing—no emails, no messages, not even a trace of his existence within the company files. It was as if Oliver had been a figment of his imagination, a phantom sent to guide him through the chaos, only to disappear when his purpose was fulfilled.

"I want a full audit on this department," Michael said sharply. "I don't care what it takes. I need to know where that money went."

Over the next few days, the team dove into the audit. As they peeled back the layers, more troubling discrepancies emerged—payments routed to obscure accounts, strange invoices from companies no one had ever heard of. The more they uncovered, the deeper the mystery grew. Every trail led back to Oliver's department, yet nothing definitive tied him directly to the missing money. It was as if the transactions had been orchestrated by someone who knew the system too well—someone like Oliver.

Michael found himself sitting in his office late at night, the worn copy of **Order in Chaos** lying on his desk, mocking him. The line from Oliver's note played over and over in his mind:

"Chaos will always return, but now you know how to face it."

Was this what he meant? A new wave of chaos, a deeper, more insidious kind?

One night, as Michael sifted through yet another pile of records, his phone buzzed with an unknown number. He hesitated before answering.

"Michael," a familiar voice said on the other end. It was Oliver.

Michael's breath caught in his throat. "Oliver? Where the hell have you been?"

"I've been watching," Oliver replied, his voice calm and unsettling. "You've done well, Michael. But there's more to learn. Chaos doesn't just come from outside forces. Sometimes, it's the things closest to you that unravel the most."

"What are you talking about? Are you behind this?" Michael's voice was tense.

"There are forces in play you can't begin to understand yet," Oliver said cryptically. "But you're getting there. Trust yourself, Michael. Trust your instincts. You'll figure it out."

Before Michael could respond, the line went dead.

He sat there, staring at the phone, his mind racing. This wasn't just about the missing money anymore. It was about something bigger, something more personal. A hidden game, a test of his ability to keep order in the face of overwhelming chaos.

Michael glanced at the book once more. The lessons were far from over, and the storm was just beginning.

He stood, looking out the window again, but this time his reflection showed not a man who had defeated chaos, but one who was still learning to master it. The challenges ahead would be unlike anything he had faced before, but he was ready.

Or so he hoped.

About the Author

Clifford Woods is a seasoned business consultant and coach with over 40 years of experience helping entrepreneurs, small business owners, and creatives overcome the obstacles of disorganization and chaotic workflows. With a commitment to fostering both personal and professional growth, **Clifford** has been a guiding force for countless individuals navigating the complexities of building and scaling their businesses.

Known for a compassionate yet results-driven approach, **Clifford Woods** specializes in creating custom solutions that bring clarity, focus, and structure to disorganized operations. Whether advising startups or established companies, the objective remains consistent: to equip business owners with practical strategies for achieving sustainable success while maintaining a healthy work-life balance.

When not working with clients, **Clifford Woods** enjoys writing, exploring philosophy, and sharing insights on time management and work-life integration. Based in Buda, Texas, he is dedicated to helping individuals and businesses thrive in an ever-changing world.

You can contact Clifford Woods through his website: https://skininthegamecoaches.com/

Don't miss out!

Visit the website below and you can sign up to receive emails whenever Clifford Woods publishes a new book. There's no charge and no obligation.

https://books2read.com/r/B-A-TZUEC-AFMAF

BOOKS 2 READ

Connecting independent readers to independent writers.

Did you love *Taming The Chaos: Business Owner's Journey to Clarity*? Then you should read *Mastering New Customer Acquisition*[1] by Clifford Woods!

Unlock the secrets to growing your small business with "Attract and Retain Customers: A Comprehensive Guide for Small Businesses." This eBook is an essential resource for entrepreneurs and small business owners who want to thrive in today's competitive marketplace.

Through practical advice and real-world examples, you'll learn how to understand your market, develop strategic marketing plans, and leverage technology to boost sales. This guide also delves into the importance of enhancing customer experience, utilizing data analytics, and forming meaningful partnerships to drive sustained business growth.

---

1. https://books2read.com/u/baR8y6

2. https://books2read.com/u/baR8y6

Whether you're just starting out or looking to take your business to the next level, this eBook will equip you with the tools and knowledge you need to attract new customers and keep them coming back. Discover how to adapt to changing market conditions and continuously improve your strategies to stay ahead of the competition.

With a clear, step-by-step approach, this guide is written in simple, layperson language, making it accessible to everyone. Don't miss the opportunity to transform your business with proven strategies and actionable insights.

About the Author:Clifford Woods, born in Belize and experienced across the globe, is a writer, consultant, and business coach with a passion for helping small businesses succeed. His diverse background and extensive experience make him the perfect guide for entrepreneurs looking to grow and sustain their businesses.

Read more at https://skininthegamecoaches.com/.

Also by Clifford Woods

Liquidations Manual
The Galactic Trouble Shooter
The Universe Within!
ALPHA SEVEN - The Silica Incident
Fun Poems
Untamed Sun
Coaching for Small Business Owners and Entrepreneurs – the Basics
Mastering New Customer Acquisition
Disorganization The Vicious Enemy of Small Businesses
Steady, Predictable Income & Business Survival
Taming The Chaos: Business Owner's Journey to Clarity

Watch for more at https://skininthegamecoaches.com/.